Storm Watch

by Mary Louise Bourget

Orlando   Boston   Dallas   Chicago   San Diego

Visit *The Learning Site!*

www.harcourtschool.com

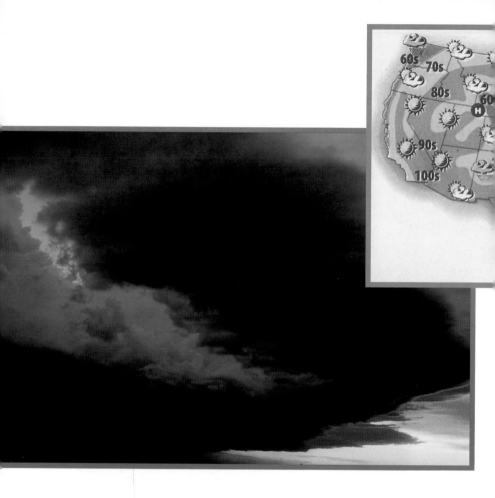

Is the sky angry? No, but these dark clouds may bring more than just rain.

Weather watchers use
lots of different maps. The
maps tell them about the
wind, the clouds, and warm
and cold air.

This radar picture shows where it is raining. It also tells how hard it is raining.

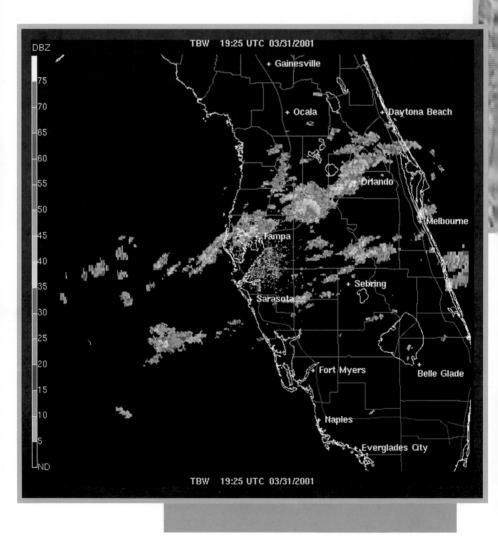

"The wind will be strong today," says the weather forecaster. "I'm sorry to say that we will have some thunderstorms."

cold air

clouds

warm air

lightning

A thunderstorm happens
when warm air and cold
air meet.

Lightning is a large spark.
Thunder comes from the
lightning. The lightning
can harm you, but thunder
will not.

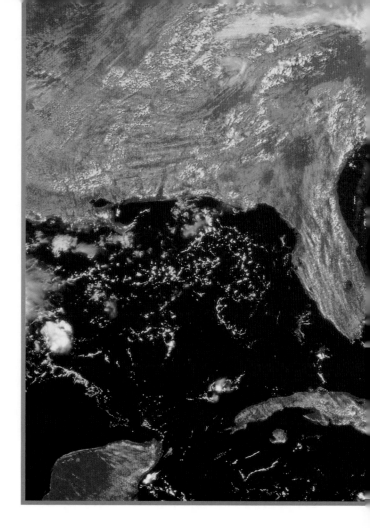

During the summer, some states get hurricanes. This kind of storm can be large.

It may cover nearly
hundreds of miles. This
hurricane was one of the
largest ever seen.

A hurricane brings very strong winds and lots of rain. Winds may take off housetops or blow down trees. A hurricane can do a lot of harm.

People need to listen to warnings about hurricanes and thunderstorms. Wind and rain together may not be safe.

If you listen to the weather forecast and learn what to do, you'll be okay.